'The Public  the Country'
The history of the Tontine Hotel, Peebles 1803–1892

Sandy
Whitnell

Copyright © 2012 Sandra Whitnell
All rights reserved.
ISBN: 9781691427628

CONTENTS

	Acknowledgments	i
1	**The Beginning** Welcome to the Tontine Context The First Trustees Clearing the site Building the Tontine	1
2	**Tontines explained** What is a tontine? The shareholders Nominees explained Management arrangements	14
3	**"The Public Rooms of the County"** The Tweeddale Shooting Club Wining, dining and dancing Politics and business Military matters	18
4	**A Coaching Inn**	28
5	**The Managers**	33
6	**The Tontine Ends**	52
7	**Postscript**	56
	Annex 1 List of original proprietors **Annex 2** 1841 list of nominees **Annex 3** Inventory of furniture and fittings	57

ACKNOWLEDGMENTS

I am grateful to the National Records of Scotland for their help in accessing hundreds of documents – see below - minutes, contracts, bills, receipts, letters, etc. relating to the Tontine Inn, and permitting some of them to be included.

And to the National Library of Scotland, whose online resource proved invaluable in accessing the newspapers of the time.

The Tweeddale Shooting Club memoir, compiled by George Wolfe Murray, furnished many details of events at the hotel, as did the minutes of the Gutterbluid club, 1823 – 1914, whose members had to be Peebles born.

Many thanks to my husband Brian for his patient help with photographs and editing.

To Kate and Gordon Innes, the current owners of the Tontine for their enthusiastic support.

And finally, to the clerks of the Tontine management committee. Without their meticulous record keeping, this history would not exist!

CHAPTER 1: THE BEGINNING

Welcome to the Tontine.

It is 1 November 1808, the opening day of a brand-new Peebles inn. The builders have left, and everything is ready.

Benoit Lenoir, a French Belgian, and his wife Margaret from Edinburgh are ready to take up tenancy. What would they have seen?

Outside is a sign and a bunch of grapes, bought from Mr Wilson in Edinburgh, for £4 9s 7d. There are four foot scrapers. The main door has a fanlight above it.

In the lantern-lit **lobby,** its floor made of polished pavement, stands a deal table, three bench seats, with 12 hat hooks on its wall.

The crowning glory of the Tontine is its **ballroom**, fifty feet by twenty feet, and nineteen feet high, the walls two feet six inches thick. Four arched windows ten feet by four feet, are glazed with best quality glass. The cornices have two enrichments and three sounding holes. The ballroom contains eight padded benches covered with red merino wool, which match the curtains, bought, at great cost, by subscription. There are steps to reach the candles.
Pic 1 and 2. The ballroom today (see page 9)

Overlooking the ballroom is the **gallery**. Two neat columns and pilasters, with either a wood or iron baluster. On it a fixed bench, and a bench for the fiddlers.
Pic 3. The gallery today. (See page 10)

There is a **supper/dining room** and a **bar** containing 12 trestles for supper room tables. (No chairs mentioned in the inventory.) Also, two sets of mahogany dining tables and three mahogany side boards. In the bar are three shelves for glasses.

Back to the lobby, where a stone stair with an iron rail and wood top rail leads down to the kitchen and passages, and up to the bedroom flat.

Upstairs, there are two beds and a grate in the **women's room,** and in the **garrets,** four beds with open fronts and bottoms. There is a **store closet,** containing shelves and a **large linen press,** a cupboard which looks like a wardrobe, in which fabric is stored horizontally.

Back down to the lobby, and from there, downstairs again to the area below the ballroom, where there are two **parlours.** Underneath the dining room is the principle **flat and bedroom,** with decorative touches such as ornamental protective plates at the keyholes.

Still downstairs, the well-equipped **kitchen,** contains a dresser, shelves, and a table at the window. Equipment includes a cylinder oven, a hagging stock, (meat preparation board) three sets of skewers. including best tinned skewers, a flaming spoon, and a tin bottle for oil.

There's a **larder** with shelves and a couple of tables, and a scullery with a lead sink. The catacombs in the wine cellar contain a bottle rack.

Outside the kitchen there is a **court[yard]** with its **small house for pigs**, roofed with slates.

A covered drain leads from the kitchen to the **stable court**.

The stable court, seventy-four by sixty-six feet, contains a pump, a well and a wooden trough.

The **stables** are equipped with two corn chests, wooden pins for hanging harnesses on, and twelve iron hooks.

And finally, a bed for the post-boy in the loft.

The whole inn, all fifty feet by forty feet of it, with its 21 pairs of window shutters and 37 doors, is ready. Benoit Lenoir, the first manager, is ready. After five years of preparation, the Tontine is finally open for business.

Context

The beginning of the 19th century was an uncertain time in the history of Britain. Much of this unease stemmed from France. The British ruling class watched the events across the channel with fear and trepidation: the execution of the French King, the French Revolution and, in 1799, Napoleon taking power. From 1803 to 1815 Britain and France were at war.

Although the war was overseas, the threat of revolution was everywhere in Britain. Historian P K. Crimmin, in *Prisoners of War and British Port Communities, 1793-1815*, estimates that there were about 122,000 French and allied prisoners of war on British soil between 1803 and 1814 alone. How many of these were dangerous republicans? Would they rouse the British to republicanism? Nobody knew. Revolution and fear of invasion was n the air.

From 1803 Peebles was a parole town, one of a number of small towns where captured French officers could live in relative comfort, having given their word to take no more part in hostilities. Other prisoners of lower rank were said to have been held in Peebles in 1798-9, probably in the town jail. And many prisoners were held in Penicuik. All this has led people to believe that French prisoners of war may have built the Tontine, and the plaque on the front of the Tontine reflects this. Yet the meticulous records at the National Records Office Scotland (NRS) do not make any reference to French prisoners being involved. There is no material evidence such as receipts or bills for their food or transportation, and no mention in the notes of any committee meetings.
Pic 4. The plaque in front of the Tontine (see page 10)

Why then build a brand-new inn in Peebles at such a tumultuous time?

The records show that from the beginning, the Tontine was intended to provide the "public rooms of the county"- something brand new and purpose built. The prime movers were perhaps inspired by the wonderful buildings of Edinburgh's Georgian New Town, including the Assembly Rooms opened in 1787.

Edinburgh had the Assembly rooms: Peeblesshire would have the Tontine.

The contract between the proprietors of the Tontine and its managers underlines this intention.

> "The ball and supper rooms...are to be used as the public rooms of the county, and particularly by the proprietors when occasion requires. The trustees have hereby reserved a right and preference thereto to be used by them at pleasure."

Surely a tenant manager would not welcome an arrangement which tied up the principal rooms in this way. Perhaps it is unsurprising that some found it hard to make the Tontine pay, as later chapters will show.

The First Trustees
It is no small undertaking to build an inn from scratch. There would be the need to commission and agree plans, get the site cleared, obtain permission to build, deal with legal matters, and commission and manage the trades involved in its building.

Sir John Montgomery, John Hay, and Robert Nutter Campbell led the enterprise. They became the trustees, responsible for handing over the Tontine to whoever became its eventual owner. They were men of status, wealth and influence, well able to start and steer through such a project, and to identify investors in the build: there were no hotel chains in 1803.

Sir John seems to have been in the lead. Born in 1766, and raised in Peeblesshire, he trained and worked as an advocate in Edinburgh, becoming M.P. for Peeblesshire between 1800 and 1831. He succeeded to the baronetcy in 1803 when he began remodelling Stobo Castle, completed in 1811. This means that he was overseeing the building work at his home at the same time as the building of the Tontine.

Pic 5. Portrait of Sir John Montgomery. (see page 11)

The second trustee was John Hay of Soonhope, a banker in Edinburgh who became the 5th baronet of Smithfield and Haystoun in 1810.

William Chambers described him as "a fine specimen of the well-bred Country gentlemen blended with the man of business."

Robert Nutter Campbell, the final trustee, was a captain of the 94th foot regiment. The eldest son of a retired planter from Grenada, he owned a number of local properties including Kailzie and Nether Horsburgh.

Clearing the site
Sir John Montgomery began purchasing the buildings on the Tontine site in 1803.

In March 1805 and April 1806, Alexander Bartram, clerk to the management committee, had to warn tenants to get out of the houses on the site.

NRS documents provide new information about these buildings and their owners, including Montgomery's 1806 petition to the Guildry Council asking permission to demolish them.

According to the petition, there were houses, a barn, a stable, and a yard near Tweed Green on the site. The petition describes these, including the names of their former owners, the state they are in, and the names of those owning adjoining properties, for example:

> " ...one little house now ruinous betwixt James Smith's house on the south, Robert Mackintosh's on the west and the High Street."

According to the petition there was a barn, a stable, and a yard near Tweed Green on the site. The petition is concerned with these buildings rather than what will be erected in its place. Perhaps it was accompanied by a sketch and measurements: Mr Oman, the local vicar, was paid to provide this in April 1806. There is, alas, no trace of any plans or sketches in the NRS records.

The Guildry Council asked three tradesmen - a mason, a wright, and a thatcher - to inspect the premises, and they reported back on Aug 12, 1806. The Council was the first effective form of building control and it continued to regulate building standards in Scotland until 1975.

> "Agreeable to minutes of council delivered to us dated 16 July 1806, we have this day examined the state of the different houses mentioned in the petition of Sir John Montgomery and others, and find the whole of said houses are one story high and thatched and we judge those in lotts one and five are totally ruinous, but all those in the other lots are in tolerable repair.
>
> "We, the underwritten, John Sanderson, William Sanderson, and Alexander Dixon, compearing before the Dean of Guild of Peebles, and being solemnly sworn, depose that the written report is just and to the best of our knowledge and belief as we and each of us shall answer to God."

Other documents in the NRS archives add to the picture of what stood on the site before the Tontine. The account of the auction of the houses is particularly interesting. The document provides the rules of the auction, held in August/September 1808, the details of the prices paid, and the names of the purchasers.

The entire structure of the properties were sold. Bartram's meticulous notes provide details of the lots by building. The notes record the names of the previous owners-Tait, who had a shop in the site, Smith, Gibson, Josh, Taylor, Grieve. Buildings included a crop barn. The fourteen lots of "Grieves front house" provide a very clear impression of the kind of property that stood there before the Tontine.

Pic 6. title page of auction of houses on Tontine site. (see page 11)

> Grieve's front house: items auctioned
> 1. Thatch
> 2. Wood of roof
> 3. Upper floor and joists
> 4. Window
> 5. Window and boards
> 6. Stair, partition and two doors

7. Whole under floor and sleepers

8. Door and shelves in rooms

9. Window in room

10. Kitchen door partition and props

11. Small press in the kitchen

12. Window in kitchen

13. Window in kitchen

14. Outer door and cheeks

The auction raised £22 15s 10d for the shareholders, reduced to £16.2s 6d after expenses.

Building the Tontine

One of the most extraordinary documents held by NRS is a detailed narrative description, 14 pages long, of the original plan of the Tontine, which had been drawn up by William Turnbull. The document is written, like the others, in elegant Georgian script with plentiful use of archaic English and Scots architectural terms. Sadly, there were no drawings.

Pic 7 First page of the Tontine specification. (see page 12).

These plans were under discussion in January 1806 and agreed by the following August, subject to the ballroom being widened by two feet. Adverts in Scottish newspapers invited bids for the building work, and by 7 October 1806, the Secretary had received six bids to build the Tontine, ranging from £2,730 to £3,205. William Turnbull's bid of £2830, although not the lowest, was accepted, provided that he wrote off the cost of drawing up the plans. £2830 is equivalent to £218,000, using the Retail Price Index (RPI) calculator.

The contract was signed on 10 November 1806. The house and the ballroom were to be roofed by July 1807 and all other buildings roofed by the end of October 1807. The inn was to be finished and the keys handed over by the 15th September 1808 "under the penalty of £500".

After four years of planning and preparation the foundation stone was laid in March 30, 1807,

> "…by the Right worshipful George Douglas of Cavers esq, provincial Grand Master of the district, when many of the gentlemen in the neighbourhood and the brethren of the Lodge of Peebles attended."
>
> *Pic 8. Report of the laying of the foundation stone. (see page 13)*

Acknowledgements of receipts during 1807 show that William Turnbull was paid in instalments, the last in July 1808.

The Tontine opened for business in November 1808.

1. The ballroom from the gallery. (see page 1)

2. The ballroom. (see page 1)

3. The gallery today (see page 1)

4. The plaque in front of the Tontine (see page 3)

5. Portrait of Sir John Montgomery (see page 4)

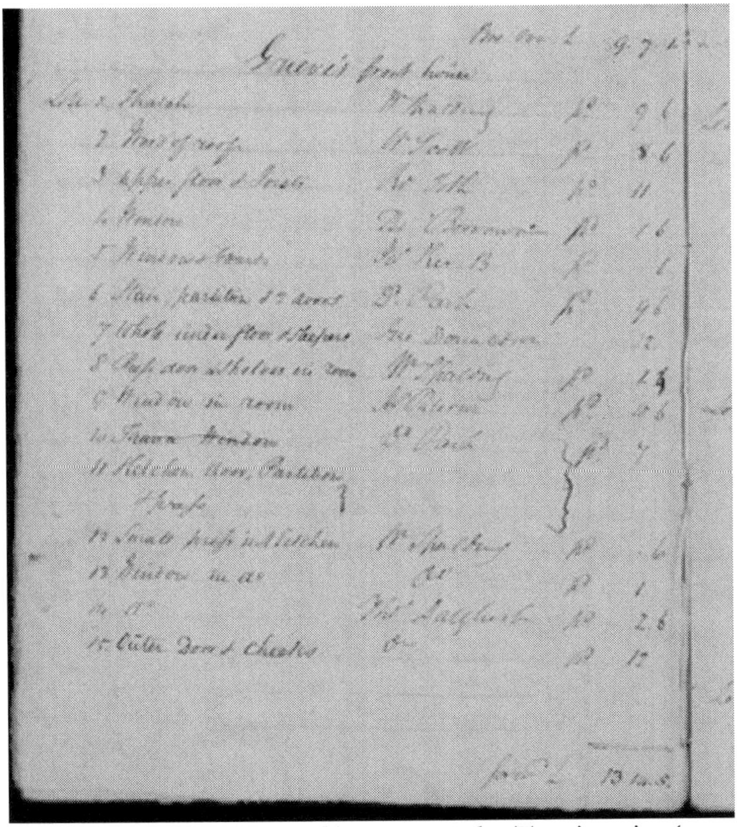

6. Title page of auction of houses on the Tontine site (see page 6)

Specifications for
building the Tontine Inn and
Offices in the Town of Peebles.

According to the Plan the Inn or principal House measures Fifty feet by Forty feet over walls, and in height for the first story, Nine feet, the second Twelve feet, the Third nine feet; which including the Joists makes in all Thirty three feet, with two Gateways as shown in the Plan.

The Ball room adjoining fifty feet by Twenty feet within walls, and Nineteen feet high from the floor to the Cieling, with a sunk Storry the same height of the Kitchen. — The sunk area

7. First page of the Tontine specification. (see page 7)

Congregation of the Bridge of Teath, gave an unanimous call to Mr Alexander Fletcher, preacher of the gospel, to be colleague and successor to his father, the Rev. William Fletcher, their present pastor.

On the 24th inst. the foundation stone of the Peebles Tontine was laid by the Right Worshipful George Douglas of Cavers, Esq. Provincial Grand Master of the district, when many of the gentlemen in the neighbourhood, and the brethren of the Lodge of Peebles, attended. A suitable address was delivered by him on the occasion, and a most appropriate prayer from the chaplain. The undertaking is on a liberal plan, and meant solely to better the accommodation of the public.

It must be particularly gratifying, and afford a source of the most rational amusement to those Ladies and Gentlemen who love the Arts, to be in possesion of a copy of Bowyer's splendid and beautiful Work of Hume's History of Eng-

8. Report of the laying of the foundation stone. (see page 8)

CHAPTER 2: TONTINES EXPLAINED

What is a Tontine?
In the early 1800s, money to build institutions such as libraries and ballrooms was raised privately. One popular method was public subscription. The Assembly Rooms in Edinburgh were financed in this way.

Peebles Tontine was funded through an investment plan known as - guess what - a Tontine, so called because it was devised in the 17th century by an Italian called Tonti.

It works like this:
People buy shares and receive dividends. Additionally, in a Tontine, shareholders name a nominee for each share they hold.

When their nominee dies, the shareholder forfeits the share.

Over time, the shares belong to fewer people, who get higher dividends.

The shareholder with the longest living nominee gets outright ownership of the property.

There was no financial benefit to being a nominee.

Shareholders could not change their nominees.

Here is an example:
There are four shares in a property.

Shareholder Adam owns three shares.
His three **nominees** are his sons: Ben, Charles and David.

Shareholder Edward owns one share.
His one **nominee** is his grandson Fred.

Ben, Charles and David die. Fred outlives them.

Edward therefore becomes the owner of the property.

Similar to a lottery, you could lose your money, but you had a chance of owning a valuable asset, in this case an inn.

Because it is dependent on the length of people's lives, the Tontine arrangement is a long-term commitment. The Peebles Tontine arrangement illustrates this: it started in 1807 and ended eighty-five years later in 1892, in a rather unexpected way, of which more later.

About the Shareholders *(sometimes called proprietors, owners or occasionally subscribers)*
The NRS records confirm William Chamber's account in "A History of Peeblesshire" that

> "The capital subscribed was £3950, in 158 shares of £25 each; altogether, the establishment cost the proprietors £4030."

There is no explanation in any record for the £80 discrepancy in the costs.

Using the increase in the RPI as a basis, this would be about £300,000 today. 75 people owned the 158 shares, many owning two or more. 32 shareholders were members of the Tweeddale Shooting Club, stalwarts of the Tontine to this day: more about them later.

The names of all the original shareholders and the number of shares they held was recorded in a contract in the NRS records. No details of nominees are provided. The full list is transcribed in **annex 1**.

Not unexpectedly, the people buying shares came from the prosperous section of society, in particular the lairds, bankers, and merchants. Many were Edinburgh based. They included eleven Merchants, eight Writers of the Silk (barristers), three Bankers, two men of the Cloth, and just three women. People who wouldn't miss the odd £25, £2,000 today, using RPI equivalence.

One notable owner was the Duke of Queensbury, "old Q," a gentleman to the bedchamber of King George III. Others of note were the Peebles provost, The Eddleston Farming Society, a mathematician, a Dowager duchess, and a baker.

Payment for the shares had to be made by Lammas 1807, before building began. Documents in the NRS archives show that shareholders were asked to pay in two instalments, and that there were some slow payers. Indeed, some were very slow payers. For example, in May 1822, James Inglis, one of the subscribers, owed £37.10s 0d of the £50 for his two shares. In embarrassed circumstances he went to the West Indies, where he died. In June 1822 the committee meeting agreed that

> "if not paid up by 16 July the names (of the people who have only paid partially) will be struck off the list"

Nominees explained

Who could be a nominee in a Tontine is specified in the contract. The contract for the Tontine Inn Peebles is probably based on one Bartram records sending for from Glasgow in 1805, which states that shareholders were

> "at liberty to enter their own life or that any other person…
> lives are confined to Great Britain and Ireland…"

The only surviving list is from 1841: there no list of the original nominees in the records. The list is transcribed in **Annex 2**. In other tontines, shareholders named public figures as nominees. But in Peeblesshire the nominees were friends, family or themselves. Bartram had difficulty in getting people to provide their nominee's details.

Shareholders could be asked to prove that their nominee was still alive, usually by producing a certificate signed by a reputable person e.g. a minister of the church. For example:

> "At Peebles the 27th seventh day of June 1840 in the presence of Robert Welsh Esq of Hopefennan and of Her Majesty's justice of the peace for the county of Peebles.
>
> "Compeared* Thomas Horsburgh Squire of Horseburgh Common, who being solemnly sworn and examined, declared in 1838, that both his nominees are still alive. All which is true as he shall answer to God.
>
> (signed)   Thomas Horsbrugh.
>   Robert Welsh JP"

Specifically, Scots law: to appear in court personally or by attorney.

Management arrangements
The shareholders' contract also outlines the management arrangements.

Sir John Montgomery, John Hay, and Robert Nutter Campbell, as trustees, held legal title until the inn was handed over to the final owner. The trustees served on a committee of seven, which usually met yearly, and reported to a meeting of the rest of the shareholders. This committee appointed the managers of the Inn, after receiving bids by would-be managers. The managers staffed and provisioned the Tontine day to day, and probably provided many of the contents. They paid a half yearly rent.

All meetings were recorded by a Writer to the Seal, starting with Alexander Murray Bartram, who was clerk to the committee. His careful record keeping has proved invaluable in providing the detail contained in this history.

CHAPTER 3: "THE PUBLIC ROOMS OF THE COUNTY"

The Tweeddale Shooting Club (TSC)
As soon as the Inn opened, the local gentry began to avail themselves of the parlours that Benoit Lenoir, the first manager, boasts of in the newspapers.
Pic 9 Advert for the Tontine 1808. (see page 26).

The Tweeddale Shooting Club made themselves particularly comfortable. It counted Lords, Baronets and Knights among its members. Many members owned shares in the Tontine, and the history of both is intertwined, so its memoir makes many references to the Tontine. The club still meets there.

Do not be deceived by the name! The full and detailed memoir has very little about hunting and shooting. The club met to dine, to drink, to plan the Tweeddale annual ball, and to do this wearing a distinctive uniform.

The club song composed in 1919 sums up the ethos of the club. It celebrates the many courses they eat; the fine wines they drink; the silver and crystal dinnerware they use; the high status of its members; and, in each verse, their coats of green.

In 1808, the club, which was established in 1790, met in the Tontine for the first time. They marked the move from the *Hottle*, now the *Cross Keys* pub, by changing the design of their coats. No longer grass green, but

> "dark (not bottle) green....and a dark green velvet collar ....
> All buttons of the coat should be silver with a pointer dog
> and the letters TSC engraved thereon."

Pic 10: Emblem of the Tweeddale Shooting Club. (see page 26)

The outfit was completed with a white vest, and black satin breeches. The rules and regulations about the uniform are extraordinarily detailed and members were fined for deviating from it.

The Tontine was a home from home for members of the club. From 1808 members could settle down to read *The London Courier*, statutes relating to poaching, and Hutcheson's *Justice of the Peace* at the Tontine for the use of members. In 1824 they added *The London Sporting Magazine*. Other publications followed.

Their magnificent silver plate and glassware was kept at the Tontine, and their wines and spirits were kept in the cellars in three special rooms, under lock and key. The club and the landlord would regularly take an inventory. One item gives us a big clue about their drinking preferences:

> "Silver plate: Eight labels with Madeira, Port, Sherry, Claret, pointer dog & TSC engraved on them – two of each kind."

The club celebrated its centenary in September 1890. Only three people attended, but they did not let the small number of attendees interfere with

> "them enjoying the excellent dinner prepared for them and thereafter spending an exceedingly pleasant evening."

The three of them consumed

> "three bottles of champagne, a Magnum of claret, a bottle of hock, a bottle of golden dinner sherry, and a bottle of liqueur brandy."

The extravagant menu for the centenary meal recorded in the TSC memoir provides an indication of the demands on the Tontine kitchen, although it appears that members of the club bought in their own servants – waiters, cooks etc. This could be why few resident servants are shown on Tontine census returns.

Pic 11 menu of the centenary dinner. (see page 27)

Wining, dining and dancing
The Tweeddale ball: Organised by the Tweeddale Shooting Club through a subcommittee, the Tweeddale ball was first held at the

Tontine on 17 and 18 October 1808 at a special opening and continued to be held there each year with few exceptions.

Preparations were taken very seriously. In 1831 the subcommittee arranged for ice and comfitures to be bought from Edinburgh, and for 120 bottles of champagne to be available. The ceiling of the Tontine ballroom was whitewashed – candles, no doubt staining them.

The *Edinburgh Evening Courant* enthused about this "splendid" ball and supper, attended by

> "upwards of a hundred distinguished fashionables ... dancing commenced at nine o'clock ...until past four."

That's seven hours of dancing.

Music was provided by Mr Spindler "with his usual excellence."

Three years later, in January 1834, the Tontine ballroom was lit by gas for the first time. The local county estates, the *Courant* reported,

> " sent forth their youth and beauty to mingle in the mystic mazes of the dance."

They had supper at one in the morning and continued to dance until late morning. You have to admire their stamina.

In 1842 the *Courant* was moved to report that

> "we have seldom seen in a county town so splendid a display of beauty and fashion."

On 10 March 1863, a ball "which was numerously attended" and a public dinner were held in the Tontine to mark the marriage of 'Bertie' the Prince of Wales to the Princess Alexandra of Denmark. According to the minutes of the Gutterbluid club:

> "The town was also illuminated in the evening. The day was unfortunately stormy and a good deal of snow which fell in

the morning marred the proceedings of the day greatly."

Other momentous events were celebrated, for example the keying in of the last arch of the bridge across the Tweed at Peebles which took place in August 1834. The procession must have been quite a sight.

> "... the members of the Mason Lodge in Peebles and deputations from Galashiels, Dalkeith, Biggar and other lodges having convened ... and being headed by a band of music from Biggar ... moved from the lodge in the Northgate to the Tontine, where they were joined by Sir John Hay of Smithfield and Haystoun, provincial grand master of Scotland, and other office bearers of the grand lodge... the magistrates, town council, and the corporation, and trades and other inhabitants of Peebles.

> "[After the ceremony] the procession moved off to the Tontine where they partook of a dinner and kept up to a late hour with great harmony."

In this account from the *Caledonian Mercury*, June 1840, the loyal toast took on an added dimension.

> "The tenants, feuers, and other friends of Lord Elibank in this part of the country assembled in the Tontine ... to render to his Lordship congratulations on the birth of a son and heir...

> "...the chairman proposed 'her Majesty the Queen' 'her illustrious consort Prince Albert' "her Majesty's ministers' etc.

> "In proposing the first toast the chairman in a very feeling and emphatic address alluded to the late attempted assassination of her Majesty. He hoped and believed that all such atrocious and villainous proceedings were abhorrent to the feelings of all classes of her Majesty's subjects. Sure he was that in this part of the country only one sentiment

obtained 'that her Majesty might long reign over a free, a religious, and an enlightened people.

"The toast was drunk with the greatest enthusiasm, and nine times nine."

The manager of the Tontine gets a great review in the article.

"The dinner, being in Cameron's, was of the best, and requires no commendation, he being well known as a first rate restauranteur."

The ballroom was not just used for dancing and meetings. In 1851 it was the venue for horticultural exhibitions, filled with flowers, fruits and vegetables in July and September. The Gutterbluid club reports that the September exhibition proved particularly successful,

"attended by all the beauty and fashion in the neighbourhood, it having been estimated that nearly 800 people visited the exhibition upon this occasion, which was altogether splendid."

August 1853 marked the beginning of the building of the railway. The grandeur of it all almost overwhelms the Gutterbluid club chronicler. Here's a taste.

"The ceremony of cutting the first turf was gone through by Lady and Sir Graham Montgomery in the presence of one of the largest assemblies of ladies and gentlemen that has ever been seen within the Royal Borough of Peebles. A marquee was erected by the directors and they entertained their friends and the representatives of the public body with wine and cake. A public dinner also took place in the Tontine Hotel when about 150 gentlemen were present.

"Altogether the proceedings of the day went off with great éclat, the day being fine and the sun shining with great splendour upon the assembled multitude..."

Presentations for sporting prowess such as rifle shooting and archery were held at hotel dinners, where

> "Toasts, song and sentiment blended to make a most pleasant and happy evening" *Caledonian Mercury October 1862*

The account in the *Mercury* of the public dinner and presentation given to Provost Todd in October 1875, tells us that

> "60 gentlemen dined in the Tontine Hotel ... a number of ladies witness the proceedings from the gallery, and an orchestra of professional musicians played appropriate music."

Politics and business
The Tontine, with its recessed cobbled square and location in the centre of Peebles High street, makes it ideally suited to public occasions both inside and outdoors. It has hosted many political and other significant events.

An insight into the election practices of the time is provided by an account from the minutes of the Gutterbluid club in 1835, when the Tontine took a central role.

> "This day Sir John Hay was elected to represent this town and county, to serve in the Reform Parliament of Great Britain. This took place at the Tontine door, he being elected unanimously by the voters who were present."

The Scottish Reform Act of 1832 had increased the electorate significantly, from 0.2% to 13% of adult males. Despite this, in Peebles, the electors

> "all dined in 6 houses opened for that purpose at the member's expense."

Locals naturally chose the Tontine to discuss nationally significant political events such as the Corn Laws, tariffs and other trade restrictions on imported food and grain, enforced from 1815 to 1846. The Anti-Corn Law League was a political movement aimed at their abolition. It was in the interests of landowners to retain them, so it is no surprise, then, that

> "... the Earl of Wemyss and March, Lord lieutenant of the county of Peebles, has called a county meeting to be held this day within the Tontine in Peebles, for the purpose of petitioning the legislature not to entertain any proposition for the altering of the present corn laws." *(London Standard Jan 1844)*

And the Tontine hosted the meeting which made the momentous decision to build a railway:

> "A large and influential meeting of nobleman and gentlemen connected with the county was held in the Tontine ballroom today to consider of a railway from Edinburgh to Peebles, when resolutions were unanimously passed highly approving of the undertaking." *Minutes of the Gutterbluid club April 1852*

In 1864 there was an attempt to abolish tolls and transfer the costs of repair of roads to landowners. Landowners objected. The Duke of Montrose addressed parliament.

> "The great promoters of road reform in Scotland were the owners of public vehicles, who ... would be entirely exempted from payment of the tolls to which they were now liable." *Hansard 1864.*

Local tenant farmers were less dogmatic: -

> "A meeting of the tenant farmers of Peeblesshire was held in the Tontine Hotel Peebles, for the purpose of taking into consideration the (road) bill ... it was agreed that without any expressing any opinion as to the general principles of the bill, or in any way committing themselves to the same, a

committee be appointed to come forward with a modification or alteration of the objectionable clauses ...." *Dundee courier* 1864

In November 1868 things got more than a little heated.

"The first election of Member of Parliament for the united counties of Peebles and Selkirkshire took place, when Sir Graham Montgomery was elected by a majority of three, against Sir John Murray of Philiphaugh who contested the seats on liberal principles.

"Great excitement prevailed in the town during the day, and upon the result being known about 6 o'clock, the windows of the Tontine Hotel were completely smashed to atoms, being the Committee rooms of the Conservatives. The smashing of the windows still continuing, Sheriff Napier appeared on the street and read the Riot Act, which had the effect of restoring quietness and dispersing the people.

"We believe that this is the first time the riot act has been read in the Royal Borough of Peebles" *Minutes of the Gutterbluid club.*

Military matters

The Tontine ballroom was host to more serious manoeuvring than merely finding a suitable dance partner. J W Buchan's History of Peeblesshire tells us that from August 1859 Peebles company of the Peeblesshire rifle volunteers held their drills twice daily in the ballroom, until their officers were appointed a year later.

They also held their two main social events there: the grand ball and the annual supper, including the presentation of prizes.

and upon the most moderate terms.
Military Knapsacks painted upon the new-improved principle, on the shortest notice.
Patterns may be seen at their Warehouse.
West Register Street, New Town.

TONTINE INN, PEEBLES.

BENOIT LENOIR begs leave to offer his most grateful thanks for the attention and patronage he has received since he opened this large and commodious Inn. The apartments are fitted up in a neat stile. The beds and furniture are new, and there are several Parlours well adapted for fishing and shooting parties. He has been careful in the selection of his WINES & SPIRITS. Travellers may rely on good stabling, and civil and careful servants.

Neat Post Chaises. The Fly for Edinburgh continues to set off at 9 in the morning. English and Scots Newspapers every day.

SUGARS.

WM. SIBBALD & CO. will expose to public Sale, at their Sample Room, on Tuesday 23d inst. at 11 o'clock forenoon.
200 Hhds. Tierces, and Barrels, MUSCOVADO SUGARS, just landed ex Mermaid, from Jamaica.

9. Advert for the Tontine 1808 (see page 18)

10. Emblem of the Tweeddale Shooting Club (see page 18)

SOUPS
Hare   Leek

FISH
Boiled Turbot   Sauce aux Homards
Fried Whitings

ENTREES
Haggis
Cotelettes de veau   Petit pois

JOINTS
Sirloin of beef   horseradish sauce
Haunch of venison   Sauce Piquante

GAME
Roast pheasants   Roast grouse
Roast partridges   Roast chickens

VEGETABLES

SWEETS
Plum pudding   Apple tart   Wine jelly

Cheese straws   celery

DESSERT
Café

Tontine Hotel   J. Mowat, proprietor

11.   Menu of the TSC centenary dinner (see page 19)

CHAPTER 4: A COACHING INN

Before the railway connected Edinburgh and Peebles, the main means of transport were coaches.

The Tontine was a coaching inn, equipped from the beginning, with a stable yard and stables, including a bed for the post boy in its loft.

It is reasonable to assume that coaches dropped their passengers at the front of the Tontine, and entered the stable yard from the rear, from Tweed Green. Early photos seem to show buildings blocking either side of the hotel.

Pic 12 Two views of rear of Tontine, probably mid 1800s. (see page 31)

In June 1842, James Cameron, the Tontine's manager from 1827 to 1843, was in partnership with Croall and Durward of Princes Street, Edinburgh. The highly successful John Croall had established his coaching and posting firm in 1820 and was awarded the Royal Warrant as "Postmaster in Scotland" in 1843

Every day coaches left Croall's offices in Edinburgh at 8:30 a.m., arriving at Peebles at 11:30 am. The coach to Edinburgh left Cameron's Innerleithen hotel at 7.15am. It stopped at the Tontine to pick up passengers, leaving at 8.30, and arriving in Edinburgh at 11.30. This of course, gave the canny Cameron the chance to sell breakfast.

The 1842 *Mercury* advert also announces that the Tontine hired out

> "Droskies, gigs, phaetons and chaises on moderate terms with first rate sturdy horses and careful drivers."

The Edinburgh to Glasgow Railway had opened for passenger traffic on 21 February 1842. The advert extolls the delights of Peebles to the residents of Glasgow, as coaches to and from Edinburgh were timed to

> "afford to Glasgow and its vicinity such an opportunity in consequence of the railway as they never before had in

visiting the justly celebrated 'St Ronan's well', 'the bush aboon Traquair', the braes of Yarrow, St Mary's loch, the Grey Mare's tail, Ashiestiel, Abbotsford, Melrose and Dryburgh, to either of which parties can go and come in less than a day."

Pic 13 advert for coaching services (see page 32)

Today most of these attractions will be familiar to residents and visitors to Tweeddale as popular places to visit. Except perhaps "the bush aboon Traquair." which was apparently a small grove of birches near the Quair, about a mile from Traquair House, and the location of a popular ballad by Robert Crawford telling a sad love story. Perhaps a trip there was the equivalent of visiting TV and film locations.

Even Rabbie Burns made the visit. The first verse goes:

> "Hear me, ye nymphs, and ev'ry swain,
> I'll tell how Peggy grieves me;
> Though thus I languish and complain,
> Alas! she ne'er believes me.
> My vows and sighs, like silent air,
> Unheeded, never move her;
> The bonnie bush aboon Traquair,
> Twas there I first did love her."

Horses were not the only residents of the stables:

> "A large elephant belonging to Batty's travelling menagerie died at the Tontine this day and was afterwards taken to Edinburgh." *Minutes of the Gutterbluid club 14 April 1856*

The minutes do not recount whether the poor creature entered Edinburgh by road or train, or what became of it after it arrived.

The coaching inn aspect of the business continued after the advent of the railways. Robert Marshall was manager of the Tontine (1869-1872) when his horses caused a serious and dramatic accident:

> "A pair of horses belonging to Mr Marshall of the Tontine Hotel ran off with the carriage to which they were attached

from the door of the hotel, and after coming in contact with the house of Mr Williamson, Clothier, they next run against the lamppost, and dragging it over, they bolted westwards along the High-street at a terrific pace, and were out of sight immediately.

"Going down Port Brae they went along Tweed Green at the same pace, and made an appearance in Eastgate, almost before the folks who had seen them start could ascertain which direction they had taken. There was a crowd collected round an auctioneer's stall in front of the corn exchange, and into it the infuriated animals rushed at the same headlong pace, smashing the stall and ware to atoms and causing serious injury to a great number of the people who was standing around it.

"James Henderson has since suffered amputation and the four others are still in a very poor state, besides others who received lesser injuries.

"The driver who had charge of the horses and who bears a good character is to be tried by sheriff and jury on the charge of culpable negligence." *Minutes of the Gutterbluid club 1 January 1870.*

The case was eventually withdrawn.

12. Rear of the Tontine (date unknown) including stable area. (see page 28)

SUMMER ARRANGEMENT
FOR THE
EDINBURGH, PEEBLES, & INNERLEITHEN COACHES.

To EDINBURGH,

ON MONDAY the 20th June, and every lawful day until further notice, a Coach will start from Cameron's Hotel, St Ronan's Well, at a quarter past Seven o'clock, A.M., and from the Tontine Inn, Peebles, at half-past Eight o'clock, allowing time for breakfast, arriving at Edinburgh at half-past Eleven o'clock.

AFTERNOON COACH

Leaves the Tontine, Peebles, at Three o'clock, arriving at Edinburgh at Six, in time for the Seven o'clock Train for Glasgow.

To PEEBLES AND INNERLEITHEN,

On MONDAY the 20th June, and every lawful day until further notice, a Coach will start from Croall's Office, No. 4 Princes Street, at half-past Eight o'clock, A.M., arriving at Peebles at half-past Eleven o'clock.

AFTERNOON COACH

Leaves No. 4 Princes Street, at Three o'clock, arriving at Peebles at Six, and Innerleithen at Seven o'clock.

The Proprietors are satisfied that in the above arrangement, they afford to Glasgow and its vicinity, &c. such an opportunity (in consequence of the Railway), as they never before had, in visiting the justly celebrated " St Ronan's Well," the " Bush aboon Traquair," the " Braes of Yarrow," " St Mary's Loch," the " Gray Mare's Tail," as also Ashestiel, Abbotsford, Melrose, and Dryborough Abbeys; to either of which, parties can go and come in less than a day.

DROSKIES, GIGS, PHAETONS and CHAISES, on moderate terms, with first-rate steady Horses and careful Drivers, can be had at Mr Cameron's Hotels in Peebles and Innerleithen.

CROALL, CAMERON, & DURWARD,
PROPRIETORS.
Peebles, June 16, 1842.

13   Advert for coaching services. (see page 29)

CHAPTER 5: THE MANAGERS

The NRS documents provide a great deal of detail about the managers between 1808 and 1857. Many letters between the manager and the committee are preserved or quoted verbatim. After 1857, however, they provide very little information. There are the usual bills, receipts etc, but little of the personal, although other sources do give us some insights. Managers after 1882 seem to have been more or less temporary appointments.

1808 - 1818 Benoit Lenoir, enemy alien
On the face of it, Benoit Lenoir was an unlikely choice as the first manager of the Tontine. He was a national of an enemy country, a French Belgian. Belgium had been annexed by the first French Republic and remained French until 1815 and the defeat of Napoleon. But here he is, being employed and accepted by Peebles Society.

Lenoir was not the only enemy alien roaming the streets. From 1798 to 1811, Peebles was a "parole" town, as highlighted by Patricia K. Crimmin in her book "Prisoners of War and British Port Communities"

Parole prisoners had to promise not to re-enter the war and were provided with the means to live in designated British towns. Some were even returned to France after making the promise. They were officers, often freemasons, and treated as gentlemen. It seems they made a welcome addition to the neighbourhood, putting on plays and getting merry with the locals. Sir Walter Scott regularly invited them to dinner and pumped them for information about Napoleon for his book. Perhaps Benoit Lenoir had the status of a gentleman, like the paroled officers.

Lenoir married a Scots lass, Margaret Millar, on 22 November 1805 in Edinburgh. The Post Office Annual Directory shows them in 1806 living at 9, South St David St, Edinburgh, just off St Andrews square, near the centre of the New Town. The Directory provided the names and home addresses of the "noblemen, private gentlemen, merchants, traders, and others, in the city and suburbs of Edinburgh and Leith." It seems that the Lenoirs were people of some standing, even though he is described as a grocer.

In September 1807, adverts in the *Aberdeen Journal* show that Lenoir "has opened that large and commodious house, lately built by Mr Gordon". The "Hotel and Tavern," in Union Street, Aberdeen, had a "choice collection of the very best wines and spirits". It also had post chaises, stabling, and "careful drivers." Although his first name is misspelled as Benette, there can be little doubt that it is the same man.

Lenoir was trading in the centre of an ambitious development: Union Street. Now a conservation area, it is described by Aberdeen council as

> "one of the engineering feats of the early nineteenth century… contains many of the City's most important and impressive buildings… one of the most important examples of early nineteenth century planned streets in Scotland."

Unfortunately, it appears that

> "Union Street's granite terraces were built to designs so inflexible and costly, that lack of occupancy, and consequently of income, was one cause of Aberdeen's bankruptcy between 1814 and 1825."

Whether it was unsatisfactory business or a better offer which led Lenoir to Peebles, cannot be known. But in June 1808 Lenoir was appointed to manage the Tontine. One year after opening in Aberdeen, the 'whole household furniture' of his Aberdeen Hotel was put up for auction in September 1808. The Tontine opened in the November of the same year.

Lenoir bid £70 per half year to manage the Tontine. There were four other bids:
- John Brighton of Peebles: £50.
- William Huntley of Mayfield Farmhouse, Peebles: £70.
- A Tylo, amount unspecified, and
- Peter Ross from Edinburgh, who offered £65, increased to £70 in a postscript. "it being always understood that the large rooms

immediately below the ballroom are to be fitted out with boxes by the way of a coffee room as formerly proposed."

Lenoir's appointment was "subject upon his producing satisfactory security to the trustees." Two people stood security for him: William Sommers of Broughton, and Richard Blackwell, vintner in Edinburgh. The contract, signed retrospectively in 1809, was for nine years from Martinmas (November 11) 1808. It is surprisingly generous. To encourage the tenant, no rent would be taken for the first three years. The rent for years four to six was to be £50, and for years seven to nine, £70. All furniture and fittings were bought and owned by the subscribers. The contract also includes the explicit reason for the building of the Tontine–

> "... that the two large rooms, viz the ball and supper rooms... were to be used as the public rooms of the county and particularly by the proprietors when occasion required. The trustees hereby reserve a right and preference thereto to be used by them at pleasure."

This requirement is repeated in each contract, potentially a hindrance to an enterprising manager.
Pic 14 Advert for new manager (see page 49)

In September 1810 Lenoir and Margaret had a son, Charles Joseph, and for a few years all seems to go smoothly. But by June 1816 Lenoir is in arrears of rent of £57.10s 5d. His wife Margaret writes to the committee about the rent, complaining that "trade at the Tontine had much decreased." She asked for a £30 rebate of the £70 rent. The committee approved, subject to subscribers' agreement.

On leaving the Tontine in 1818, Lenoir and family went back to France, as reported in the obituary of his wife Margaret Lenoir, in the *Caledonian Mercury* of September 1849. Margaret was

> "long and honourably associated with the Tontine of Peebles... retired with her husband and son to France, where she remained till their deaths about 12 years since, when she returned to her own country."

Among the charitable bequests are one of "the sum of £500, the interest of which is to perpetuate an annual allowance to five creditable burgess's widows of the town of Peebles." That's about £50k today, a surprising amount given the later difficulties at the Tontine. She left £100 for food for the poor of Stirling, where she was born, and £50 to the Strangers Society, particularly for the natives of Belgium. There is no mention of any surviving children.

Pic 15 Margaret Lenoir's bequests. (see page 49)

1818 - 1827 Peter Ross: A family business

In 1817 Benoit Lenoir's lease was coming to an end. The Tontine was advertised for let, but only one bid was received – from Benoit Lenoir. A year later, in September 1818, they advertised again: this time four offers came in. Peter Ross's bid of £70 per half year secured him a 9½ year lease from Martinmas 1818. Someone called Peter Ross had bid unsuccessfully against Lenoir in 1808. William Ross, presumably a relative, and manager of the (at present unlocated) AMCA ironworks stood surety for him.

Lenoir left the Tontine on Whitsunday, 1818.

Ross and his guarantor signed a detailed inventory, now transcribed with help from the *dictionary of the Scots language*, see **Annex 3**. The inventory offers some fascinating insights into the interior of the Tontine.

Of particular interest is the "bunch of grapes at the main door", presumably the emblem of an establishment which sells wines. Also the sedan chair in the servant's hall. The details of the ballroom are especially interesting. Chambers reports that the curtains were paid for by subscription, and the NRS papers list the names of the subscribers. The curtains were made of merino wool, in red, with eight matching bench seats. The gallery which overlooks the ballroom had an apron in the same material, as well as a bench for fiddlers. There is something oddly satisfying about knowing the colour of the curtains in the Tontine over 200 years ago.

During 1819/20, whilst Peter Ross was still an active manager, the Tweeddale Shooting Club memoir notes that he agreed that a press, (a large cupboard, probably one built into a recess in the wall), should be kept exclusively for their silver plate etc in room 9. The inventory shows that there was a dresser there.

In May 1823, Ross asked that management of the Tontine be assigned to his son William and unnamed eldest daughter. The committee agreed, "provided that if (the daughter) marries she forfeits the rights of the assignation. " No reason is given for the request, and no intimation about what Ross would be doing instead.

At the 1823 meeting the secretary reported a dividend of nine shillings per share, (or £36, using the increase in RPI as a basis.)

Perhaps the son and daughter were not as successful as the father. By July 1827 the Inn was not so profitable, and Alex Williamson, appointed secretary on the death of Alexander Murray, reported that there would be no dividend until Whitson 1828, as "any sum to be divided before that time so trifling as not to be worthy of effort."

In August 1827 the articles and conditions of lease show that William Ross was the de facto manager when the lease expired at Whitson 1828.

1827 – 1843 The entrepreneurial Cameron

James Cameron was one of the longest serving of all of the Tontine managers and seems to have been the most entrepreneurial.

He previously managed a Hotel in Dunfermline called the *Spire*. It was an important public building, built in 1807 as a Guildhall and linen exchange. By 1816/17 it had become the Spire Inn. Now called The Guildhall & Linen Exchange, it is a Wetherspoons hotel and pub.

In September 1827 he wrote, with an offer of £70.

> "… if the offerers are requested to attend at the opening of the offers on 2 October next, will thank you to give notice of this, and I shall attend this."
>
> *Pic 16 Cameron's bid: for the Tontine. (see page 50)*

He had already tested the lie of the land:

> "Mr Cameron has applied to me (John Gibb) respecting the Tontine of Peebles and I beg leave to refer him to you as the best-informed person on the subject…He has been led to believe that the advertisement of this inn is a manoeuvre to raise the rent upon the old tenant, in which case he would not make an offer…"

He was not the only one trying to tap into the old boy network. One of the five rivals for the post was William Thompson from Glasgow, who writes to Sir James Montgomery at Stobo Castle,

> "Sir.
> … I have every reason to believe that you were a particular friend of my late father who lived in Peebles… I am now tenant of the Vine hotel and Tavern in this city and from my long experience in the public line, flatter myself (if I am fortunate enough to get the situation) that I will conduct the business of the Tontine Peebles to the entire satisfaction of the nobleman and gentlemen …. Hoping that your good self will excuse the Liberty of this addressing you… "

The decision was deferred because "some of the offers were not sufficiently explicit" and the let re-advertised. A month later two bidders, including William Ross, withdrew their offers. Cameron upped his offer to £100, and on 3 November 1827 accepted the terms of the lease.

Cameron was keen to get the Tontine into first class shape – standards seem to have slipped when William Ross was in charge. And he wasn't above a bit of plain speaking, as can be seen from a letter sent to Bertram, and reported to the committee in June 1828, when he

> "begs to observe that in expectation the house would be properly cleaned by whitewashing and painting, he was induced to offer a considerable sum of more than he at one time contemplated."

He complains that nearly all the rooms

"have not been painted for several years, and consequently have not that clean and comfortable and respectable appearance, which the outward aspect of the Inn would infer."

He is also concerned about the state of the stables – '

"even at this dry season of the year the stables on the east side of the square …are inundated with water… it is a very material object … that the stables are in a good and sufficient state."

He asks

"that the committee will forthwith direct this evil to be remedied without delay."

But he doesn't just want the Tontine to be spick and span: Cameron has big plans for improvement. He wants to add another bedroom or two, and enhance the facilities by introducing baths:

"…the want of baths in this place has been much felt and … invalids at Peebles and Innerleithen and the country around find it necessary to repair to Edinburgh for the use of them…he would propose … to convert the room [under the ballroom] into an apartment for baths …which he has no doubt would be found of essential benefit to the Inn…"

Not just any baths. He

"proposes to bring up the mineral water from Innerleithen every morning, which with the baths would be a great additional accommodation to the public and the inhabitants of the Town…"

He suggests keeping the cost down

"by enlarging the present henhouse and converting the same into a washing house (the want of which there being none is very inconvenient) with a boiler therein from which the baths could be supplied with warm water."

The Committee agrees to these improvements, costed at £168 (about £13,000 using RPI.)

In 1833 he complains that "the roof is now a complete wreck", and seems exasperated with the work of the builder, Turnbull.

In 1839 the committee agrees that the "two parlours which form the supper room" should be painted French grey, in oil, the windows painted, new fenders and irons ordered for the supper rooms and the old ones removed to the "commercial room."

The improvements continued: According to the *Memoir of the Tweeddale Shooting club*, the Peebles annual subscription ball of 10 January 1834 "was brilliantly lighted up with gas for the first time." Electricity arrived in 1928.

He was not averse to a bargain. The TSC on inspecting their cellar describe four of their bottles of champagne as "bad." Cameron takes it off their hands for 2/6d per bottle.

From 1831, the letters of poet James Hogg, the "Ettrick Shepherd," show that Cameron also ran St Ronan's Inn at 12 Piccadilly Street, Innerleithen. The Inn had, among its other attractions, an artificial curling rink. This is confirmed by an advert in *the Scotsman* of August 1834:

> "To all keen curlers: as the dinner to the Ettrick Shepherd takes place in the Tontine Peebles on the 19th current, Prof Wilson in the chair. Mr. Cameron the landlord begs to inform all curlers that he has prepared a handsome silver medal to be played for on his artificial link in Innerleithen on the day following. Competitors must be on the ice at precisely 11 o'clock and as this is the first thing of its kind in this country, great sport is anticipated."

Cameron was based at the Tontine: at the time of the 1841 census he lived there with his wife, Jane, three young children, and the staff: a barmaid, four servants and a waiter. Three of the servants have common local names: Brodie, Sait and Dalgleish. In 1842, he still owned both inns, and hired out coaches from both establishments.

In June 1843 Cameron gave up the Tontine and left for Innerleithen, an event recorded in the *Caledonian Mercury*. A dinner was held by "numerous and highly respectable party of friends from the town and neighbourhood." to celebrate his leaving. He was paid "a well merited compliment" which met "most marked applause."
It was clearly a most enjoyable evening: "various other toasts were given, and the company did not separate till a late hour."
Pic 17 Cameron's farewell dinner. (see page 51)

1843 - 1850 Andrew Forbes: ice and water.
The contract with Forbes, as well as affirming the shareholders' priority call on public rooms, also refers to a wine cellar being reserved for their use.

The relationship with the Tweeddale Shooting Club continued. From 1845 to 1850, TSC brought in a cook, Mrs Thompson, from Edinburgh to cook dinner at a pound per dinner and three shillings for her coach fare: it may have also brought their own servants to wait at table.

In 1846 Forbes got into trouble for failing to procure a supply of ice for the club dinner.

Peebles was modernising, and there were consequences. The 1845 Management Committee meeting sanctioned payments to the water company to lay on water to the Tontine, noted as 'part of the general improvements to the Burgh.' As a result, the 1846 Committee meeting was asked to meet the costs of the Tontine's water rates, as water was no longer free.

The Tontine continued as a coaching Inn, William Steel and Co providing from 2 Princes St, Edinburgh "elegant four – inside post coaches to Peebles Tontine and Mrs Riddell's Hotel Innerleithen at 4.00pm daily."

1850 – 1851 The soon to be bankrupt Charles Fraser

Charles Fraser was by far the shortest serving manager of the Tontine. Appointed in November 1849, with "good reports of his character and ability", a standard contract was issued in early 1850, to expire in 1857.

In 1850, the hotel had undergone some repairs. The main cost, of £144, was for Lithgow Purdie of Edinburgh to paint the hotel. At the same time the "first" bedroom was converted into a parlour for commercial gentlemen, and "a boiler erected outside for boiling the horses meal."

In the March 1851 census, 23-year-old Fraser, from Perth, and his wife Mary are shown at the Tontine with a servant, a cook, a chambermaid and a hostler. But by August that year, the *Scotsman, Glasgow Herald, London Morning Post, Hampshire advertiser*, and *Dundee Courier*, all report the same thing.

> **"Scots bankrupts:** Charles Fraser, hotelkeeper Tontine Hotel Peebles. Creditors meet in said Tontine hotel, Peebles 29 August and 20 September at 1 o'clock."

The ignominy! Not just to go through sequestration, but for the meetings to be held in the very same hotel.

The committee minutes in November 1851 show that Fraser 'and the trustee for his creditors,' had left the Tontine on the 18 October, having auctioned off his belongings a few days earlier.

Without a manager the Tontine was vulnerable, and the secretary reported that it had been

> "forcibly entered by thieves on the 15th ultimo after the roup [auction] of Fraser's effects and some articles of trifling value having been abstracted…"

As a result, he had

> "engaged a family to reside in and protect the hotel till a new tenant's entry at the rate of seven shillings per week."

This unfortunate development left the proprietors in a difficult position. An urgent advert appeared in the Scottish press:

> **"Desirable hotel to be let with entry immediately**
> The Peebles Tontine Hotel will be let for such period as shall be agreed on, with entry immediately. The premises are remarkably well situated, containing every convenience, and ample accommodation for carrying on an extensive business, and are an excellent repair..."

There is a possible sighting of Fraser in the 1861 census. A Charles Fraser, of the same birthplace and of the right age, is recorded as living in Dirleton. He is described as a trainer of racehorses and has three children under five with his wife Mary. His brother in law is a jockey. It is to be hoped that this career was more successful than his time at the Tontine.

1851 – 1857 The Bullish Thomas Noble

The committee meeting that noted the departure of Charles Fraser also considered the offers received as a result of the urgent advert for a new manager. The committee, consisting of Sir G Montgomery, John Erskine, esq. of Venlaw, and the Provost of Peebles.

Offers were received from Duncan MacPherson and Thomas Noble. Duncan MacPherson will feature later.

> "Mr Noble," the secretary reported, "had stated his capital to amount to £500, and that Mr Rampling of the Waterloo Hotel Edinburgh was willing to assist him to such further extent as might be necessary for properly furnishing and commencing business. "

The committee appointed Thomas Noble, and by December 1851 he was agreeing the inventory.

He seems to have been an outspoken man, as demonstrated by a letter to the secretary of the committee barely six months after taking the tenancy:

> "Dear sir,
> I beg to call to your attention the dilapidated state of the chimney cans on the Tontine chimneys, for the last two days we have been nearly smoked out of the house. Something must be done to put them in a proper state of repair. Unless they are attended to immediately in this stormy weather, the cans that remain, if left in their present state, may do more damage than the sum required to put them right.
>
> "I may also mention to you that the kitchen range is in a very bad state of repair, in fact it is useless for cooking purposes and to mend it in its present state would be throwing money away. You would oblige me by ordering some tradesmen to look at it and see what can be done to make its fit for use.
>
> "I am dear sir your most obedient servant
>
> Thomas Noble.
>
> "PS the window curtains that we're awaiting and the glass shades for the gas which were broken (entered in the inventory as completed) have not yet been replaced. Will you be kind enough to give orders for their being so."

A new kitchen range was not fitted until 1858.

Noble's rent would be due on Martinmas, 11 November. In November 1853 he wrote:

> "I was disappointed both on Tuesday and yesterday in getting money that I expected and having purchased a rather large stock of whiskey and brandy previous to the

rise in price, I am short of ready cash at present. You would do me great favour if you will not press for any rents for a day or two.

I have some money to get in and I will pay you as soon as possible. Wishing that you will accede to my request I am dear sir etc etc"

The records do not show if the delay was accepted.

Two years later, in November 1855 he is again behind with the rent and exhibiting his bullish nature:

"Dear sir
I understand your clerk called **again** [*my emphasis*] today for my rent.

I have been confined to bed for the last four days and I am not yet able to go out. Else I would have been down, as I wish to see you. If it makes no difference to you, I will call next week and settle. If this will do, please to let me know."

The lease was not renewed.

1857 - 1869 Successful John Smith

John Smith was born in Borthwick in 1820. According to the TSC memoir, he came from the Star hotel, Haddington. This is confirmed in the 1855 valuation rolls, where Smith is recorded as the tenant at the inn. The Star "was long known as a respectable hostelry."

The Star still exists, as one of the buildings in the centre of Haddington renovated to create the John Gray Centre, which houses the Archives and Local History Centre for the county. One of its rooms is called the Star Room.

The 1861 census shows Smith living at the Tontine with his wife Anne and their two-year-old daughter Elisabeth. There have four resident servants.

In 1871 he still lives in Peebles with his wife and child Elisabeth, and a servant, now in "Tweed Green house". It looks as if John was successful at the Tontine: he is described as a farmer of 54 acres – and their home has 16 rooms.

1869 - 1872 Robert Marshall and his "household effects"

Probably the youngest son of a gamekeeper in Dunbar (1841 census). The 1871 census has him living in the Tontine with wife Isabella and two young children, both born in Edinburgh. Also resident are three female domestic servants and a male waiter. One of the servants, Annie Searson, is shown as being born in Calcutta India. The influence of the British Empire stretched near and far.

We know little of his time at the Tontine, but when Marshall left, he auctioned off his "household effects." The inventory of items provided by the proprietors has already been discussed: now we have, in the form of an advert for the auction, the detailed account of what the manager was expected to provide. The inventory completed for the auction helps us to imagine what the rooms would have looked like at that time.

The auction included
- "Brussels carpets," a type made of coloured woollen yarns drawn up in uncut loops to form a pattern.
- One of the parlours contained a "very superior" telescope dining table which seated 14, perhaps used by the Tweeddale Shooting Club?
- From the lobby, a "beautiful stained lamp," and a "Percha" door mat, which, according to Wikipedia, is a kind of latex, used so extensively during the second half of the 19th century that it became a household word.
- "An eight-day American clock," so called because it only needed to be wound up once a week.
- The furnishings for ten bedrooms were sold, including two "Elizabethan mahogany beds."
- The dinner service of 160 pieces in green and gold, described as "very excellent and beautiful," in addition to twelve dozen cups and saucers, dozens of forks and spoons (but no knives) trays, tea pots etc.

- In the "miscellaneous" section we find "a wagonette to hold 5" and "a small bus to hold 4 inside," an "oak salting tub", a "pigeon house", a "corking machine", and a "bottle rack to hold 26 Dozen"!

Pic 18 Extract from advert for sale of Marshalls effects (see page 51)

1872-1878 Duncan McPherson – a hero?

In March 1872, Duncan McPherson, from Kingussie, described as an hotel keeper from Innerleithen, applied for a "certificate for the sale of exciseable liquors" for the Tontine Hotel. He would have been 54 years old.

The 1861 census shows that he is running the Station Hotel, Peebles, with his wife, Mary. All his children, aged from 3 to 13, were born in Peebles, so we can reasonably assume that he resident in Peebles for at least 13 years, ie from 1848.

It may be that he had managed Peebles inns for some time: the Gutterbluid minutes record that in a fire in 1850 at the Crown, "six valuable horses were got out at the great risk of the landlord Mr McPherson cutting their harnesses while the fire was raging about him."

1878 - 1882 Nova Scotian Michael Power

Michael Power came a long way to manage the Tontine – from Halifax Nova Scotia, Canada, according to the census records. Why or when he arrived in Scotland is unknown. His wife was Scottish, born south of Edinburgh. In 1861 he was living in Edinburgh with three young children, his two eldest born in Haddington, and working as a cab driver. In 1871, still in Edinburgh, he is working as a messenger and has two lodgers.

The 1881 census shows him managing the Tontine with the help of 3 servants, including a post boy. In 1882 he moved back to Haddington to take over the George hotel, (which still exists). By 1901, a widower, he had retired to St Andrews with his daughter Emma.

1882 – 1886 Elizabeth Cruickshank

In the 1886 edition of Slater's Commercial directory, Mrs Cruikshank is named as "proprietress" of the "Tontine & posting house; head-quarters of the Bicycle & Tricycle Touring Clubs." The association with cycling is interesting as the Tontine still maintains a strong connection to highly successful cycling festivals held in and around Peebles.

Also in 1886 is an announcement in the *Glasgow Herald* of the death of William Fraser Cruickshank, "late of Ceylon" aged 33, at the Tontine. So perhaps Mrs Cruickshank left when her husband or son died.

1887 – 1888 George Leith
At present there is no information about this manager.

1888- 1892 John Mowat
An advert on 5 May 1888 describes the Tontine as being under new management, and a coaching inn, in spite of the railway. It also includes the cost of staying there: £2. 12s 6d per week equivalent to £288 weekly, using RPI, and £1 equivalent to £105 for Saturday to Monday.

Glasgow, 9th October, 1851.

DESIRABLE HOTEL TO BE LET,
With Entry Immediately.

THE PEEBLES TONTINE HOTEL will be LET, for such period as shall be agreed on, with entry immediately. The Premises are remarkably well situated, containing every convenience, and ample accommodation for carrying on an extensive business, and are in excellent repair. They were erected, not with a view to profit, but to supply good accommodation for the County Gentlemen, and parties attending the usual Fairs and Markets, for Commercial Gentlemen, and for Tourists and Sportsmen, for whom the surrounding district contains many well-known attractions; and the Proprietors have resolved that in selecting a Tenant, Rent will not be a chief object, but that the selection will mainly depend on the character and ability of the party.

For particulars, apply immediately to Stuart & Blackwood, Writers, Peebles.

Peebles, 2d October, 1851.

TO COTTON OR WOOL SPINNERS, OR PAPER-MAKERS.

14. Advert for new manager (see page 35)

of London early next month.

CHARITABLE BEQUESTS.—We lately announced the death of Mrs Le Noir, 4, Albany Street, North Leith, who many of our readers may yet remember—her name being long and honourably associated with the Tontine of Peebles, which Sir Walter Scott refers to in "St Ronan's Well" as the "New Hotel," opened by the deceased and her husband, who formed then the modern rivals of "Meg Dods." Mrs Le Noir left Peebles upwards of thirty years ago, and retired with her husband and son to France, where she remained till their death, about twelve years since, when she returned to her own country. Amongst a large number of bequests, she has left the sum of L.500 sterling, the interest of which is to perpetuate an annual allowance to five creditable burgess's widows of the town of Peebles—L.150 to the poor widows of the Hammermen, of the Society of Hammermen of the town of Stirling—L.100 to be expended in the purchase of coals and oatmeal, to be distributed in four successive years, to the poor of the town of Stirling, being her birth-place. L.50 to the Edinburgh Royal Infirmary—L.50 to the (Edinburgh) Indigent Gentlewomen's fund—L.50 to the Strangers' Society—particularly for the natives of Belgium, the birth-place of her husband—L.50 to the Established Church of North Leith, part of which to assist in purchasing a small library for the use of the children of the Sabbath schools, in which the deceased took a great interest for some years.

15. Margaret Lenoir's bequests. (see page 36)

> Dunfermline
>
> Sir I enclose sealed offer for the Sim
> Public, If the offerers are requested to attend at
> the opening of their offers on the 2d Oct next I
> will thank you to give notice of this and
> I shall attend but if I do not hear from
> you I shall understand it is not necessary
> for me to attend and shall expect to hear
> from you in the event of my offer being
> accepted   I am Sir Yours &c
>   James Cameron
>
> Spire Hotel
> 24th Sept 1827

16. Cameron's bid for the Tontine. (see page 37)

DINNER AT PEEBLES.—Mr Cameron of the Tontine Hotel, Peebles, was, on Tuesday the 23d ultimo, entertained at dinner by a numerous and highly respectable party of friends from the town and neighbourhood, on the occasion of his leaving that establishment for the far-famed village of Innerleithen. James Alexander, Esq. Happrew, discharged the duties of the chair; the Rev. Thomas Adam and the Rev. Alex. Thomson officiated as croupiers. After the usual loyal toasts, the Chairman called for a bumper, and in a very neat speech, in which he paid a well-merited compliment to Mr Cameron, proposed his health and wished great success to him at Innerleithen. The toast was received with the most marked applause, and Mr Cameron returned thanks in appropriate terms. Various other toasts were given and songs sung in the course of the evening, and the company did not separate till a late hour.

17. Cameron's farewell dinner. (see page 41)

There will be SOLD by PUBLIC ROUP, on TUESDAY, 21st MAY 1872, the whole FURNITURE, HOTEL FURNISHINGS, HOUSEHOLD EFFECTS, &c., of the TONTINE HOTEL, PEEBLES, belonging to Mr ROBERT MARSHALL, the outgoing Tenant.

PARLOURS—Telescope Dining Table to dine 14, very superior; Circular Mahogany Table on Pillar and Claw, Couch and 6 Chairs and Easy Chair, in rich Crimson Damask; Small Mahogany Table, Walnut Work Table, Card Table, Whatnot, Brussels Carpets, Rugs, and Crumbcloths; Mirror, Curtains, Poles, and Rings, &c.

BED-ROOMS—The Furnishings of 10 Bed-Rooms, consisting of 2 Elizabethan Mahogany Beds, in Crimson Damask; Iron Chair and Cushions, 10 Iron Beds, 5 Double Bedsteads, 5 Single do., 11 Mattresses, 11 Palliasses, 2 Feather Beds, Bolsters, Pillows, about 30 Pairs Blankets, a quantity of Bed and Table Linen, 21 Chairs, 7 Dressing Glasses, 3 Dressing Tables, Towel Rails, 3 Baths, 3 Chests of Drawers, Chamber Ware, Carpets, Rugs, Fenders, Fireirons, &c.

PUBLIC ROOMS—Dining Table, 8 ft. 3 in. by 4 ft. 4 in.; Square Mahogany Table on Pillar, Oblong Mahogany Table, Birch Pembroke Table, 12 Mahogany Chairs in Haircloth; 24 Strong American Chairs, very suitable for a Hotel; Spanish Mahogany Sideboard (open, 7 ft. 3 in.), Sofa, Writing Desk with Drawers and Press, very useful; Mahogany Cabinet, with Book Shelves; Mirror, Carpets, Crumbcloths and Rugs, Curtains, Poles, and Rings, Fenders, Fireirons, &c. &c.

LOBBIES—Clock, Beautiful Stained Lamp, Chairs, Large Gutta Percha Door Mat, Waxcloth, Matting, Stair Carpets and Rods, Umbrella Stand, &c.

KITCHEN AND HALL—Eight-Day American Clock, Large Tea Infuser with Cran, New Deal Table, suitable for a Farmer's Kitchen; 2 Tables, with Trossels; Forms, 2 Hotplate Screens, Mangle, Clothes Screens, about 20 Dozen Pots and Pans, various; Bottle Press, &c. &c.

18. Extract from advert for sale of Marshalls effects. (see page 46)

CHAPTER 6: THE TONTINE ENDS

The end of the Tontine

Earlier, this history looked at how the finances to build the Tontine were raised - by using a tontine. To recap, shareholders identified a nominee per share, and when their nominee died, the share was forfeit. Shares could be passed down or sold, but nominees could not be changed.

We learned that at the beginning of the Tontine, that 75 people owned 158 shares, and each had a nominee. Each year between 1840 and 1870 the Tontine's management committee recorded the number of surviving nominees. 95 nominees were alive in 1840. In 1870, sixty-two years later, there were still 35. How long could this tontine last? Many nominees had been adults when the shareholders submitted their names. Would any of the shareholders have predicted that the tontine arrangement would still be in place all these years later?

The remaining shareholders ran out of patience before they ran out of nominees. The decision to sell the Tontine was made in 1885, ie midway through Mrs Cruickshank's management, and before Leith and Mowat ran the hotel.

Who had the longest living nominee? Who became the sole proprietor, the beneficiary of the tontine arrangement? The NRS holds the papers of the Sprot family of Haystoun, Peeblesshire, which include the final legal papers detailing the sale of the Tontine. They make interesting reading.

The papers show that in 1887, some 80 years after the tontine was set up, two nominees were still alive: William Forbes, nominee of Sir Adam Hay: and John Gardner Lyell of 93 Lorraine Road, Holloway, nominee of Major George Lyell. *Myheritage.com* records a John Gardener Lyell born in Scotland in 1806 and passing away in 1888: the dates fit. William Forbes is as yet unidentified.

The two remaining shareholders came to an agreement and contracted in July 1887:

> "That instead of awaiting the natural termination of the tontine, should, with our consent as the holder of the two remaining shares, bring said subjects to a public sale and divide the proceeds between us respectively… "

So the Tontine would be sold, and the proceeds split.

The NRS papers include a document dated September 1888, which values the hotel at £3500. There is also a description of the hotel to be used in an advert for its sale.

It seems that the price did not attract a buyer, although they tried several times to sell it. In April 1889 an advert appeared in the *Glasgow Herald* offering the Tontine for sale at the reduced price of £1750.
Pic 19 Advert for sale of the Tontine. (see page 55)

It describes the hotel as being

> "For upwards of eighty years the principal (hotel) in Peebles."

It was sold at a loss on the 1888 valuation price, for £2130. Both shareholders received £1043 14s 9d. or using the RPI calculator, £109,700 each. This was their return on the purchase of a £25 share in 1806.

There is no explanation as to why the hotel was purchased for more than the asking price, perhaps contents and stock were included.

1892 – 1926 The tontine is dead – long live the Tontine!

William Borthwick and Duncan McPherson took over the Tontine at Whitsun 1892. (There is a discrepancy in the date of purchase: the contract between the shareholders states that the hotel was sold to Borthwick and McPherson in May 1889.) For the first time, the Hotel was in the hands of an owner manager.
Pic 20 Advert for Borthwick's Tontine. (see page 55)

A Duncan McPherson had bid to manage the Tontine in 1851: and had actually managed the Tontine from 1872 to 1878.

It appears from the 1892 advert that McPherson worked with Borthwick at the Commercial Inn and joined him at the Tontine, operating as a postmaster from the stables. The two men are named in the contract as the purchasers of the Tontine.

Borthwick was an experienced hotel worker and a long-term resident of Peebles. Born in 1855 in Forteviot, a village in Strathearn, he married Ellen, nee Marshall, sometime between the 1881 and 1891 censuses. Ellen was born in 1860, in Canonbie, Dumfriesshire.

The 1881 census shows him working as a stableman in an unnamed Peeblesshire High Street hotel for Isabel Andrews. His future wife Ellen, and her sister Agnes, four years her junior, also work there.

By the 1891 census Borthwick is running the Commercial hotel, (now called The County), which is two doors away from the Tontine. He and Ellen, now married, have two daughters, Isabella Agnes and Mary Ewart. Agnes was also living and working there, and they have two servants.

The 1901 census shows the Borthwicks in the Tontine. with two more children: Janet Newton and William Hugh, the first son. There seems to be a nurse to look after the children.

Borthwick, a keen fisherman, ran the Tontine until his death in Oct.1905, when his widow, Ellen, took over. She continued to own – and run it, perhaps until 1920. She died in 1923. There is a memorial to them both, and their daughter Janet, in Peebles churchyard.

This history ends with the purchase of the Tontine by a national chain in 1920, which ran the hotel until it was purchased by Kate and Gordon Innes.

Which makes them only the second owner managers in the Tontine's long and interesting history.

PEEBLESSHIRE.

DESIRABLE HOTEL FOR SALE

For SALE, within Dowell's Rooms, No. 18 George Street, Edinburgh, on Wednesday, 10th April, at One o'clock Afternoon,

The TONTINE HOTEL, PEEBLES, containing Dining and Drawing Rooms, Coffee-Room, 2 Bar Parlours, 2 Sitting-Rooms and 8 Bed-Rooms, also Large Ball-Room, and ample Kitchen and Servants' Accommodation. The Offices comprise Stables, containing 19 Stalls and 1 Loose Box, 3 Coach-Houses and Harness-Room, and Coachman's House, &c.

The Hotel, which for upwards of eighty years has been the principal one in Peebles, occupies an excellent site in the High Street. The Ground in front of the Hotel forms part of the Property.

A considerable sum has recently been spent in improvements, and the Subjects are in good order.

REDUCED UPSET PRICE, £1750.

For particulars, apply to Messrs W. & W. Blackwood & Smith, Writers, Peebles, who have the Titles and Articles of Roup.

19. Advert for the sale of the Tontine Apr 1989. (see page 53

Classified Ad 275 -- No Title
The Scotsman (1860-1920); Apr 16, 1892; ProQuest Historical Newspapers: The Scotsman pg. 11

PEEBLES.—TONTINE HOTEL and POSTING ESTABLISHMENT.

I beg to intimate that I enter this Hotel at Whitsunday Next. The OLD-ESTABLISHED BUSINESS of DUNCAN MACPHERSON, JOB and POST MASTER, will continue under my charge, but from and after the above date at *Tontine Stables only.*

WILLIAM BORTHWICK.

COMMERCIAL HOTEL, PEEBLES, April 1892.

N.B.—Letters and Telegrams please address "Tontine" after Whitsunday.

20. Advert for Borthwick's Tontine. (see page 53)

Postscript

In January 2018 the Borthwicks returned to the Tontine, this time as guests. The family were celebrating the 90th birthday of George Borthwick, the grandson of William and Ellen. His father, William Hugh, was born at the Tontine, (see above) and it was the first time the family had visited.

A very special moment.
Pic 21 The Borthwicks at the Tontine

21. The Borthwick family with the author at the Tontine

ANNEX 1
LIST OF ORIGINAL PROPRIETORS

Rt Hon Sir James Montgomery of Stanhope Bart
John Hay of Soonhope, banker in Edinburgh
Robert Nutter Campbell of Kailzie.
Samuel Anderson banker in Edinburgh
Thomas Allen
John Anstruther
Alexandra Allen of Glen
Alexander Brodie of Langside
John Burton of Ladyurd
James Burnet of Barnes
James Burnett of Barnes younger
James Bartram writer in Edinburgh
Robert Brunton merchant in Leith
Gavin Bengo merchant Edinburgh
Alexander Campbell of Granada
Thomas Cranstoun ws
Sir Thomas Gibson Carmichael of skirling Bart
James Crichton Esq collector of customs, Irvine
Col Alexander Dickson of Hartree
Captain Andrew Douglas at Hartree
The Right Hon Alexander lord Elibank
The preses of the Eddleston farming society
John Erskine esq of Venlaw
The Right Honourable Lord Forbes
Sir William Forbes of Pitsligo Bart
The Rev Charles Findlater, minister of Newlands
William Fraser merchant in Edinburgh
William Govan of Hawkshaw
Sir James Hay of Smithfield Bart
Capt James Hay of the East Indian [navy?]
Alexander Horsburgh Peebles
Thomas Horsburgh, younger of Horsburgh
Arthur Hogue of Calcutta
Robert Hay of Drumzelier
James Horne of Langwell WS

Alexander Henderson merchant, Edinburgh
Mrs Hart of Castlemilk
James Pye Inglis merchant, leith
Rev Alexander Ker minister of Stobo
James Ker merchant, Peebles
Miss Anne Ker at Kerfield
John Ker WS
William Loch Younger of Rachan
William Laidlaw of Hyndhope
Mr William Laidlaw, mathematician
Miss Barbara Montgomery at Kailze
Robert Montgomery barrister at Law
The hon Capt Alexander Murray of Elibank
Colin McKenzie of Portmore
James Wolfe Murray of cringletie, advocate
William Murray of Henderland
Sir George Montgomery of Magbiehill
Aeneas McKay of Scotstoun
Robert Dundas McQueen of Braxfield
William Murray writer Edinburgh
Hugh Mitchell merchant Musselburgh
Patrick Maxton banker Edinburgh
John Murray advocate
Sir James Nasmyth of Posso, Bart
Gideon Needham at Durnhall mains
James Ker Provost Peebles
Alexander Pringle at Innerleithen
Rt Hon his Grace William Duke of Queensberry
Alexander Steuart at Haystoun
Peter Sanderson
Lawrence Tweedie of Oliver
Walter Williamson of Cardrona
Robert Welsh Younger of Mossfennan
Alexander Welsh at Herstone
Anthony Wilkinson merchant Edinburgh
Charles Young merchant in Edinburgh
The Countess Dowager of Hyndford
Andrew Turnbull accountant
William Turnbull Baker Peebles
James Turnbull Wright in Peebles

ANNEX 2
1841 LIST OF PROPRIETORS AND THEIR NOMINEES

Samuel Anderson, Banker Edinburgh:	Adam Anderson his son
Alexander Allan Late of Glen:	George Allen his fourth son
William Aitchison of bordand[?.]:	Helen Aitchison his daughter
	David Aitchison his son
William Aitchison Jr of bordand:	Himself
James Aitchison, St Clements Wells:	Himself
Trustees of John Anstruther of Airdel:	Right hon Earl of Traquair
Alexander Brodie, Galashiels:	Himself
Charles Brodie, Innerleithen:	Himself
Reps of the late J Barton Of Stewarton:	John Craig his nephew
William Barnett:	Son James Barnett Of Barnes
Christian Catherine Barnett Of Rothesay:	Herself
Trustees Robert Branton, Merchant Leith:	James Thomson, son of John Thomson insurance broker Edinburgh
Trustees of Gavin Bengo, Merchant Eburgh:	Barbara Bengo his daughter
Roberts Nutter Campbell, Of Kailzie:	Himself
	Mrs Campbell his wife
	Miss Ann Caroline Campbell
	Miss Ann Hart daughter of Major Hart of Castlemilk
	Miss Jane Horsburgh daughter of Alex Horsburgh of Horsburgh
	Miss Ann Burnett daughter of GP Burnett of Barnes
	Robert N Campbell son of John Campbell of Armadale
	Miss Margaret Hart daughter of major Hart
Heirs of Alexander Campbell, Haylodge:	Mungo Campbell his son
	Elizabeth Campbell his daughter

	Helen Campbell ditto
Sir Thos Gibson Carmichael of Skirling:	Thomas McKay son of? Scotstoun
	Eleanor Richardson daughter of ? Richardson Kirkconnel
Sir George Clark Of Pennycuick Bart:	Himself
	Miss Clark his sister [
Reps off Arthur H Cushing[?], Peebles	Arthur Cushing his father
Right hon Lord Elibank:	Hon George Murray his son
	Miss Mary Murray his daughter
Eddleston farming club:	John Brydon son of Wm Brydon late of Orchard mains
John Erskine of Venlaw:	Himself
Heir of late Sir Wm Forbes of Pitsligo:	Jane Forbes eldest daughter
	Sir John Stewart Forbes Barnett
	Honourable Walter Forbes his second son
William Fraser, Merchant, Edinburgh:	William Fraser his son
	Lord Elcho son of Earl of Wemyss
William Gordon Of Hallinyre:	Himself
John Horsburgh, Baker Edinburgh:	Himself
Sir Adam Hay Baronet of Haystoun:	Miss Mary Hay his sister
	Elizabeth Hay his sister (now Lady Blair)
	Jane Hay (now Mrs MacKenzie Frazer)
	Charles Murray Hay his brother
	Samuel Hay his brother
	Charles Hay Forbes son of the late Sir William Forbes Baron
	David Anderson son of Samuel Anderson of Rochester

	Capt James Hay late of the Coutts East Indiaman
	James Hay son of Col Hay
	Miss Mary Hay
Late Alexander Horseburgh of Horsburgh:	Helen Forbes daughter
Thomas Horseburgh of Horsburgh:	Mary Nisbet Horsburgh his daughter
Donald Horne W.S. Edinburgh:	Himself
Late Robert Hay of Drumelzier:	William Hay his eldest son
Mrs Major Hart of Castlemilk:	James Montgomery her eldest son
Hall & Burn, wool merchants Fisherrow	Helen Hall daughter of Alexander Hall
Mrs Margaret Dicksonon, Stow	Herself
Lady Spittal, Edinburgh	Herself
Mrs Ann Ker or Cummin Glasgow	Herself
Late John Ker, WS:	John Richardson some of William Richardson, brewer Edinburgh
William Lock of Machen:	Stuart Lyall Second son of ditto
William Low, accountant Edinburgh	John Brown of Coulter Mains
Ditto	Robert Somerville son of William Somerville, Gormiston town
Sir Graham Montgomery of Stanhope	James Hall, son of Sir James Hall of Dunglass
Ditto	Elizabeth Hall daughter ditto
Ditto	Catherine Hall daughter ditto
Robert Montgomery of?	Himself
Ditto	Montgomery Hart, eldest son of Major Hart
Late Lord Elibank, formerly Capt Murray, trustee	Lord Elibank
William Mackenzie of Portmore	Mrs MacKenzie his mother
Ditto	Himself
William Murray of Henderland?	Himself
Ditto	Himself
Eneas Mackay of Scotstoun	Helen McKay his daughter
Catherine Greig, relict of David Greig:	Herself

Archibald Montgomery of Whim:	Charlotte Montgomery
Ditto	Anna Nash London
Heirs of ? Wolfe Murray of Cringletie:	Lady Stewart of Allenbank
Hugh Mitchell 4 St Andrews Square Edinburgh:	Himself
Burgh of Peebles:	John Ker, son of late Provost James Ker
Ditto	Janet Marshall daughter of Bailie Marshall
Peter Sanderson, banker Edinburgh:	Thomas Sanderson his eldest son
Alexander Stewart, Forbes and Co. bank:	Himself
Tweeddale Shooting and Coursing club:	John Archibald Murray advocate.
Lawrence Tweedie of Oliver:	Lawrence Tweedie son of Thomas Tweedie
William Turnbull, stamp office Peebles:	Elizabeth Park, daughter of late Mungo Park
Andrew Turnbull accountant of London:	Margaret Leckie, daughter of late rev Thomas Leckie, Peebles
Late Walter Williamson of Cardrona:	Walter Williamson of Grenada
Robert Welsh of Mossfennan:	Himself
Andrew Wilkinson, merchant Edinburgh:	Anthony Wilkinson his son
Charles Young, merchant Edinburgh:	Archibald Boyd, son of William Boyd merchant, Leith

ANNEX 3
"INVENTORY OF FURNITURE AND FIXTURES IN THE PEEBLES TONTINE PROVIDED BY AND BELONGING TO THE PROPRIETORS, 1818"

Kitchen
A grate, fender and two irons complete.
A Cellander {cylinder?] Oven
A boiling table, complete.[1]
A kitchen dresser, and table at window.
A smoke jack complete.[2]
Two large double skewers.
Two balancing ditto and a flaming spoon[3].
Two small ditto
A hagging stock
Shelves in the kitchen, and scullery.
4 Foot scrapers at kitchen door.

Larder
A fixed table at window.
A moving table and shelves.

Women's room
Two beds.
A grate.

Cellar
A bottle rack. – a large ditto
Three game tressles in ditto.

Servants hall
A deal table.
Three forms ditto
12 cloak pins

---

[1] Seems to be a hob, fuel not specified.
[2] https://commons.wikimedia.org/wiki/File:Smoke-jack.jpg
[3] Possibly a flambé spoon

A Grate fender and fire irons.
A knife board in passage.
A Sedan chair and lifters

Low Bow Room
Grate fender and fire irons.

Middle room
Grate, fender and fire irons.

Water closet
Water closet completed

Room number one
Grate, fender and fire irons

Bar
A Press
Three shelves for glasses.

Room number two
Store closet in landlord's room.
Grate fender and fire irons.
Shelves and drawers
A large napping press in ditto

Room number three
A grate fender and fire irons.
A sideboard in ditto.
Brass lustre

Room number four
A grate fender and fire irons
A sideboard in ditto.
Brass lustre
Two sets of dining tables, mahogany.

Lobby
6 bells and two below, cranks and pulls.
A glass lanthorn.

Ditto for staircase.
A Globe lamp at main door.
A tin bottle for oil.
A sign board.
A bunch of grapes at main door.
14 supper room tables.
Two additional deal tables for ditto.

Room number five
A Grate fender and fire irons.

Room number seven
A Grate fender and fire irons.

Room number eight
A Grate fender and fire irons.

Room number nine
A Grate fender and fire irons.
A Mahogany sideboard in the same.

Ball room
Eight stuffed forms.
3 brass lustres
Six brass Branches for Gallery
Steps for [4]lustres
12 hat hooks.
Five window curtains complete, red merino[5]
Eight merino covers for forms.
Merino apron for gallerys
A chest in the gallery for curtains.
2 forms in ditto for fidlers.

Garret Rooms
4 Grates fenders and fire irons.

---

[4] *https://en.oxforddictionaries.com/definition/lustre* A prismatic glass pendant on a chandelier or other ornament. 'a chandelier dripping with glass lustres'.

[5] Merino is a type of wool.

4 fixed beds in ditto with open fronts and bottoms

Stables
2 corn chests
Window pins for hanging harness on.
12 iron hooks for ditto.
A bed for the post boy, in loft.
A cast iron pump in court.
3 ladders.

Force pump at the back of coach house

[Signed by] Peter Ross, William Ross, William Thomson, Vine Tavern – 31 Maxwell St Glasgow

Printed in Poland
by Amazon Fulfillment
Poland Sp. z o.o., Wrocław